OCT 2 3 2019

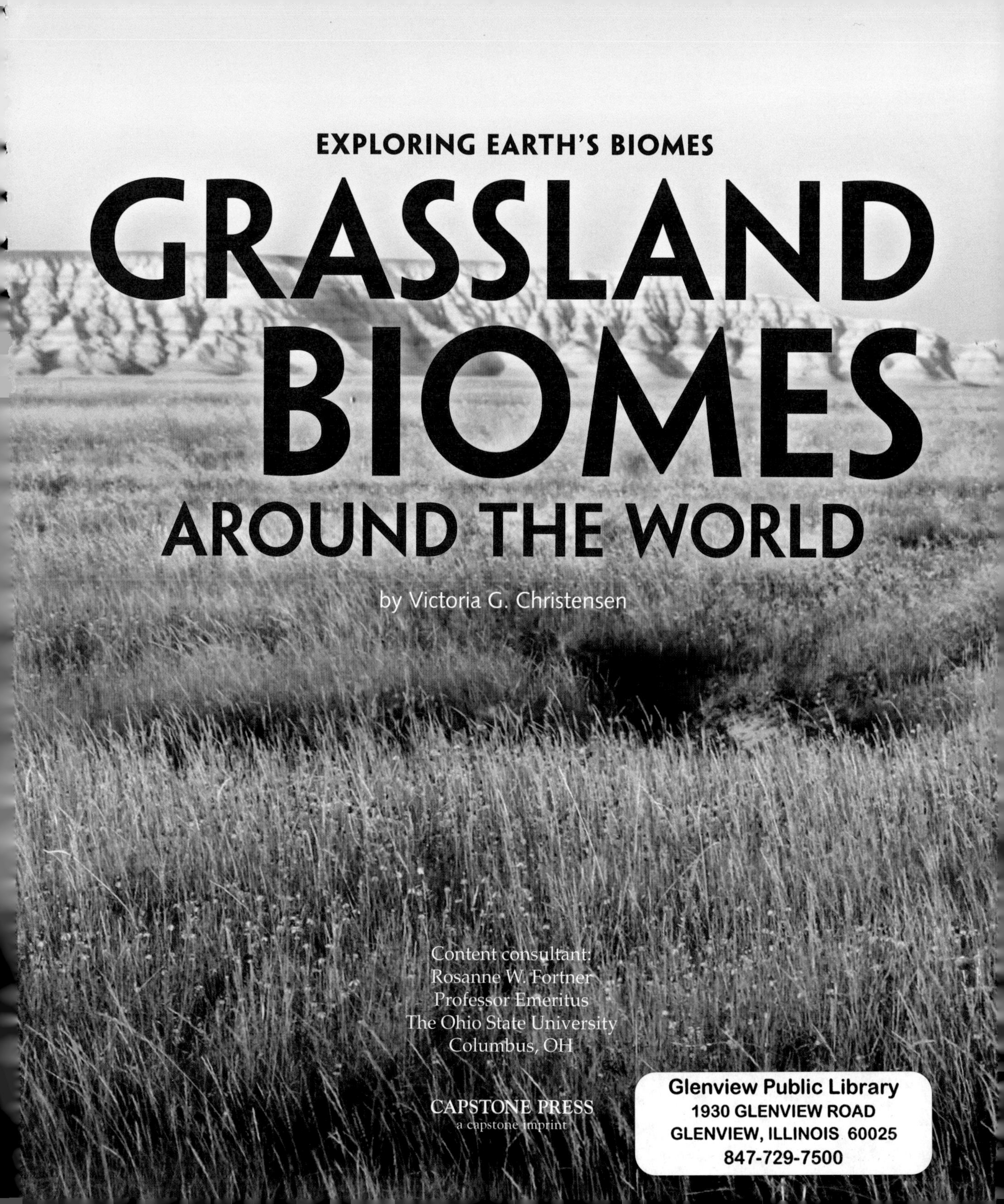

EXPLORING EARTH'S BIOMES

GRASSLAND BIOMES
AROUND THE WORLD

by Victoria G. Christensen

Content consultant:
Rosanne W. Fortner
Professor Emeritus
The Ohio State University
Columbus, OH

CAPSTONE PRESS
a capstone imprint

Fact Finders Books are published by Capstone Press
1710 Roe Crest Drive, North Mankato, Minnesota 56003
www.capstonepub.com

Library of Congress Cataloging-in-Publication Data
Names: Christensen, Victoria G., author.
Title: Grassland Biomes Around the World / by Victoria G. Christensen.
Description: North Mankato, Minnesota: Capstone Press, [2020] | Series:
   Fact Finders. Exploring Earth's Biomes | Includes index. | Audience:
   Age 8–9. | Audience: Grade 4 to 6.
Identifiers: LCCN 2019002050| ISBN 9781543572131 (hardcover) | ISBN
   9781543575347 (paperback) | ISBN 9781543572186 (ebook pdf)
Subjects: LCSH: Grassland ecology—Juvenile literature.
Classification: LCC QH541.5.P7 C475 2020 | DDC 577.4—dc23
LC record available at https://lccn.loc.gov/2019002050

Editorial Credits
Gina Kammer, editor; Julie Peters, designer; Morgan Walters, media researcher;
Kathy McColley, production specialist

Photo Credits
Getty Images: Laurie OÂ¹Keefe, 12; iStockphoto: pierivb, 7; Science Source: Carlyn
Iverson, 15, TIM BROWN, 5; Shutterstock: aaabbbccc, background 4-5, 6-7, 8-9, Bibek
Ghosh, bottom 18, Designua, bottom 20, dikobraziy, 27, Dmitry Pichugin, bottom
6, background 10-11, 12-13, 14-15, Doug Matthews, top 25, Durden Images, top 29,
Gabrielle Ewart, (girl) Cover, Jason Patrick Ross, background 1, 3, 30-31, 32, Jo Jones,
bottom 22, Katiekk, bottom 19, Kit Leong, background 22-23, LMspencer, top 21,
Menno van der Haven, 26, MicroOne, top 9, Muangsatun, bottom 14, Nic Keller,
top 17, Niv Koren, background 16-17, 18-19, 20-21, Romrodphoto, middle 16, Tom
Alyea, background 24-25, 26-27, 28-29, turtix, top 11, Vertyr, (grass) Cover, Zurijeta,
(mountains) Cover

Printed in the USA.
PA70

TABLE OF CONTENTS

CHAPTER 1

WHAT IS A GRASSLAND BIOME?

The sky seems to go on forever! You can look in any direction for miles and see no trees or bushes. It might just seem like a lot of grass, but this place is teeming with life. You are in a grassland biome.

The grassland biome is one of five main biomes. Biomes are large areas that have certain types of climates, plants, and animals. The five main biomes are aquatic, forest, desert, grassland, and tundra.

Grasslands have many names—prairies, pampas, steppes, and savannas. They are all areas where rain isn't predictable. Grasslands receive more rain than deserts and less rain than forests. The rainfall in a grassland doesn't support many trees.

Grasslands are covered in plants that can survive **drought** and fire. These plants can even keep growing after being nibbled to the ground. Large animals such as bison, zebras, and antelopes **graze** here. Grasslands also support millions of birds, insects, and bacteria hidden in the grass. People live in grasslands too—about 800 million people around the world. All these living things have **adapted** to the grassland biome in their own ways.

The five main biomes can be further broken down into more specific biomes.

FACT BOX

Some scientists estimate that grasslands cover about 25 percent of Earth's land area. Grasslands are found on every continent except Antarctica.

coniferous forest

desert

marine

Mediterranean

mountains

polar

steppe

temperate broadleaf forest

temperate grassland

tropical grassland/savanna

tropical rainforest

tundra

adapt—to adjust to particular conditions
drought—a long period of weather with little or no rain
graze—to eat grass and other plants

TROPICAL GRASSLANDS

Grasslands are divided into two main groups, tropical and temperate. Tropical grasslands are also called savannas. They receive 20 to 50 inches (51 to 127 centimeters) of rain per year. The warm climate allows grasses to grow tall. Many people live in savannas. Farmers grow hardy crops or graze livestock.

a savanna in Uganda, Africa

giraffes in Africa's eastern tropical grassland

SAVANNAS

Savannas are located near the equator. They are hot and dry. India, Australia, and Africa all have savannas. Animals living in savannas include emus, kangaroos, zebras, and elephants. In Africa, elephant grass grows to about 10 feet (3 meters). People cook it in stew or feed it to their livestock.

TEMPERATE GRASSLANDS

Temperate grasslands are found in North America, Europe, South America, and Asia. They are called prairies, pampas, or steppes and receive 10 to 30 inches (25 to 76 cm) of rain per year. Grasses tend to be short and grow in the warm season. But during the colder months, plants are **dormant**. People live here because of the good soil for crops. Also, the grasses are good for grazing cattle.

PRAIRIES

Prairies cover the large open areas of North America. Some are tallgrass prairies. Others are shortgrass prairies. Tallgrass prairies are wetter and better for growing crops. Shortgrass prairies are ideal for ranchers to graze cattle. Other animals in these grasslands include bison, coyotes, and gophers.

PAMPAS

In South America, treeless plains are called pampas. Guinea pigs, giant anteaters, and **guanaco** live there. Sometimes cold winds from the south meet warm air from the north. Then storms called pamperos produce heavy rain and strong winds.

Cowboys in the pampas are known as gauchos. They herded cattle across the pampas until European farmers arrived and turned much of the pampas into croplands.

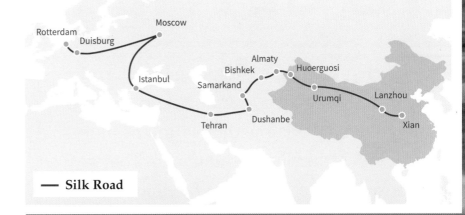

— Silk Road

For thousands of years, people traveled on camels or horses along the Silk Road that connects Asia to Europe. Parts of it were large stretches of flat grassland that made travel easy. People traded silk, tea, and spices. Some Silk Road trade routes are still used today.

STEPPES

The steppes of Europe and Asia are much like shortgrass prairies in North America. Many people living on the steppe are **nomads**. They herd cattle, using the vast steppe as a food resource. Other animals include camels and argalis, which are large mountain sheep with huge, curling horns.

dormant—when growth slows down or stops
guanaco—an animal resembling a llama that lives in the pampas
nomad—a person who moves from place to place to find food and water, rather than living in one spot

CHAPTER 2

LIVING THINGS WORKING TOGETHER

Each grassland has unique plants and animals. To keep grasslands healthy, plants and animals work together. Humans must work with other living things too. That's because we all compete for food and space.

Let's look at an example from the North American prairie. At one time, as many as 60 million bison roamed there. Bison stir the soil with their hooves, keeping it healthy.

Bison supplied food, leather, and other resources to Native American families. Hunting bison was an important part of their lives. These families also used roots and other parts of prairie plants for food and medicine. For example, they used the purple coneflower to treat snakebites, bee stings, and toothaches.

bison eating grass in Custer State Park in South Dakota

However, people didn't always take good care of the grasslands. European settlers came to the prairie and plowed much of it to plant crops. The bison were overhunted. By 1889 only about 1,000 bison were left. Today people use land more carefully. Nearly 500,000 bison now roam in national parks, as well as on farms and the open prairie.

A LOOK UNDERGROUND

Imagine looking out over a grassland region. What lives there? What would you see if you got close? A snake might slither through the grass. You also may see gophers, voles, or prairie dogs.

Prairie dogs dig a network of connected tunnels.

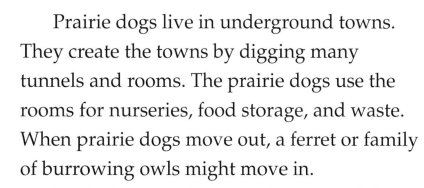

Prairie dogs live in underground towns. They create the towns by digging many tunnels and rooms. The prairie dogs use the rooms for nurseries, food storage, and waste. When prairie dogs move out, a ferret or family of burrowing owls might move in.

Look closer, and you might see a ladybug or a grasshopper resting on a blade of grass. Earthworms squirm from the soil. Dig with a shovel to find worm tunnels. The worms help churn the soil. The holes allow air and rain to get to plant roots.

Grasslands are also filled with millions of things you can't see. Fungi and bacteria are key parts of grasslands. They are called **decomposers**. They recycle waste from the food chain. Waste turns into soil **nutrients** that farmers need to grow thriving crops.

FACT BOX

Prairie dogs are a keystone species, meaning they support other grassland plants and animals. But the prairie dog population has shrunk by more than 95 percent in North America! This is a problem for the more than 150 other species that rely on prairie dogs for survival.

decomposer—a living thing that breaks down natural material
nutrient—a substance that plants and animals need for good health

DEEP SOILS AND DEEP ROOTS

Plants play an important part in the grassland life cycle. Bacteria help plants decompose. Then the rotting plants slowly form new soil with more nutrients. Plants soak up the nutrients through their deep roots. The recycled nutrients help plants grow.

Fires are also important to grasslands. Fires were common in grasslands before people built towns and farms on them. A grassland fire might start from a lightning strike. The wind spreads the fire rapidly. Fire burns invading plants or seedlings. It also cleans out thatch, which is dead plant material that settles near the plant roots. Rain and sunlight can then reach the roots of native plants. The deep roots help plants survive fires. The fire's ashes add even more nutrients to the soil.

prairie fire

There's more to grasses than what's on the surface. Lawns and crops have shallow roots. But grassland plants have very deep roots that hold the rich soil in place.

Temperate grassland soils are rich and deep. Early people soon learned the value of this rich soil for growing crops. Around 12,000 years ago, farming gave people a reliable food source. Some hunter-gatherers built permanent homes, changing human society.

CHAPTER 3

A VAST RESOURCE

People rely on grasslands. Even the smallest part of the biome is important to human survival.

BUSY BUGS

About 900,000 different kinds of insects live on Earth. They make up most of the world's animal species. Insects such as bees and butterflies are **pollinators**. Many grasses, flowers, and crops need to be pollinated to grow. People began keeping bees many centuries ago and still do today. They enjoy the honey the bees produce, and the bees also help pollinate their crops.

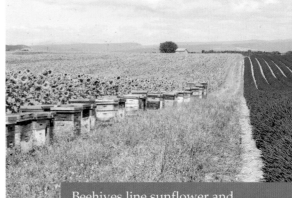

Beehives line sunflower and lavender fields in France.

FACT BOX
Scientists have estimated that 10 quintillion individual insects live on Earth. That's 10,000,000,000,000,000,000! Just one grassland region may contain 1,000 insect species.

A ladybug eats aphids.

Many insects are food for larger animals. For example, giant anteaters in Brazil dine on termites. Some people eat grassland insects too. Insects are packed with vitamins and protein. In Africa, kids might munch on fried locusts as a tasty snack.

Ladybugs are also good for grasslands. They eat small **aphids**. Aphids leave behind a sticky substance that allows fungus to grow on plants. This fungus can destroy an entire crop.

aphid—a tiny bug that sucks sap from plants
pollinator—a living thing that moves pollen from one part of a plant to another, allowing the plant to form seeds

SOARING BIRDS

Vultures are a common grassland bird. They are **scavengers**. They might seem disgusting because they eat dead animals. They thrash their wings and dig in with bloody talons. They stab their beaks into the rotting flesh. But vultures have an important job. They quickly clean up dead animals. A vulture can eat more than 2 pounds (0.9 kilograms) of meat a minute. By consuming these dead animals, vultures reduce the spread of disease by flies or bacteria.

griffon vulture

People hunt birds in many grasslands. On the Mongolian steppe, nomads use falcons to hunt small animals such as foxes. Hunting animals with birds of prey is called falconry. The falcons help the nomad survive by hunting small game. Nomads on the steppe rely on animals for all their food and clothing. Fox fur can be made into warm coats. Nomads even use the animal's **dung** to make fires.

A falcon lands on its trainer's arm.

FACT BOX

Peregrine falcons are found in many biomes, including forests, wetlands, and tundras. They also live in grasslands, where some stay during **migration**. This falcon can dive for prey at speeds faster than 199 miles per hour (320 kilometers per hour)!

dung—solid waste from animals
migration—the regular movement of animals as they search different places for food
scavenger—a living thing that eats dead or rotting animals

ROAMING ANIMALS

Large animals are key resources in grasslands. They affect where people live and how they survive as people follow or live near them. The African savanna is a good example. It doesn't have many large towns. Many people who live there are nomads, ranchers, or hunter-gatherers. They raise or hunt the large animals for food.

Wildebeest are prized by hunters. More than 2 million wildebeest migrate clockwise around the savanna each year. They follow the rains and the green grasses. Hunters then follow the migration of the animals.

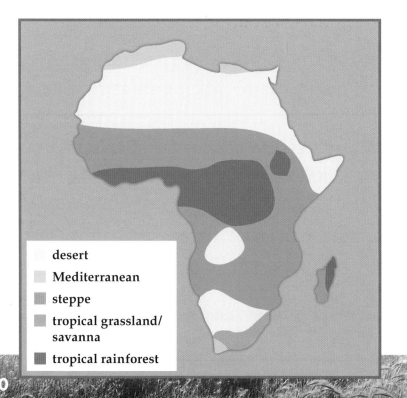

desert

Mediterranean

steppe

tropical grassland/
savanna

tropical rainforest

Large animals are part of the natural balance of grasslands. Wildebeest and other animals such as giraffes are **herbivores**. They eat the grassland plants. Just as wildebeest eat hardy grasses, giraffes eat the leaves of acacia trees scattered around the savanna. In turn, **carnivores** such as lions eat the wildebeest and giraffes. After a lion eats, vultures or other scavengers might eat the leftover flesh. Then bacteria and termites show up. They break down what's left and create healthy soil.

carnivore—an animal that eats only meat
herbivore—an animal that eats only plants

CHAPTER 4
FEEDING THE WORLD

Huge, flat grasslands with few trees are perfect for crops. Farmers are drawn to the rich, healthy soil. When tractors and other farm machines were invented, grasslands began to change. Tractors could easily plow fields. Tall grasses became fields of wheat and barley.

Rows of trees border flat open fields in England.

BUSTING SOD

When settlers first moved to the North American prairie, they needed homes. But the lack of trees made building a traditional house difficult. Instead, settlers used what they had available. Many built houses of sod, which is the grass-covered surface of the ground. The grasses' roots helped hold the soil together. Another common type of house was a dugout, made by hollowing out the side of a hill.

THE NEED FOR WATER

Farmers began growing crops such as corn on the plowed grasslands. Corn needs a lot of water. It grows well in years with lots of rain. But in drier years, farmers need to **irrigate**. They dig ditches, bury pipes, or use large sprinklers to bring water to the fields. Some farmers use underground water from wells. Sometimes the water sprays from a sprinkler, creating a circular pattern.

FACT BOX
The prairies of North America are often called the "world's breadbasket" because much of the wheat made into bread grows here. A bushel of wheat has about 1 million individual kernels, weighs about 60 pounds (27 kg), and makes about 90 loaves of whole wheat bread.

irrigate—to supply water to crops using pipes or channels

CHAPTER 5

A BIOME OUT OF BALANCE

Grasslands are especially at risk because water is scarce. When too much water is drained for farmland use, prairie ponds shrink. This action disturbs bird migration and harms plants and animals.

When too many animals graze on grasslands, the grasses might not grow back. Grazing and farming have destroyed much of the savanna.

Lack of water and overgrazing aren't the only issues. Many people apply chemicals to their crops to kill insects and help the plants grow. But these chemicals can kill native plants and harm wildlife.

FACT BOX
The Sahara Desert is spreading into and covering part of the African savanna each year.

prairie pond

Grasslands also decline when people build communities. After people move in, wildlife disappear because their habitat is gone.

Due to these factors, many grassland animals are **endangered**. This includes the black-footed ferret, whooping crane, and some elephants. Even more plants and bugs are at risk. For example, the American burying beetle is endangered. When this little insect finds a dead animal, it digs a hole to bury the animal's body. This process gives nutrients back to the soil. This beetle used to be common, but now has vanished from many areas.

endangered—at risk of dying out

BLOWING IN THE WIND

Winds also present a challenge for grasslands. When gentle breezes blow across the grasses, they ripple just like water. The wind picks up seeds and blows them across the land. The seeds settle into the rich soil. The wind also carries pollen, helping pollinate many grassland plants and crops.

But the wind isn't always gentle. There aren't many trees to block large gusts. And many grasslands are flat, with few hills to block the wind. This factor makes grasslands the perfect place for thunderstorms and tornadoes. These heavy storms can be a problem for farmers who are trying to keep the rich soil in place.

A storm moves across open land.

Some farmers plant rows of trees called windbreaks between fields. Windbreaks help block wind and reduce erosion. But recently many people have cut down windbreaks to make more room for crops. Some scientists think that if we aren't careful, there might be another Dust Bowl.

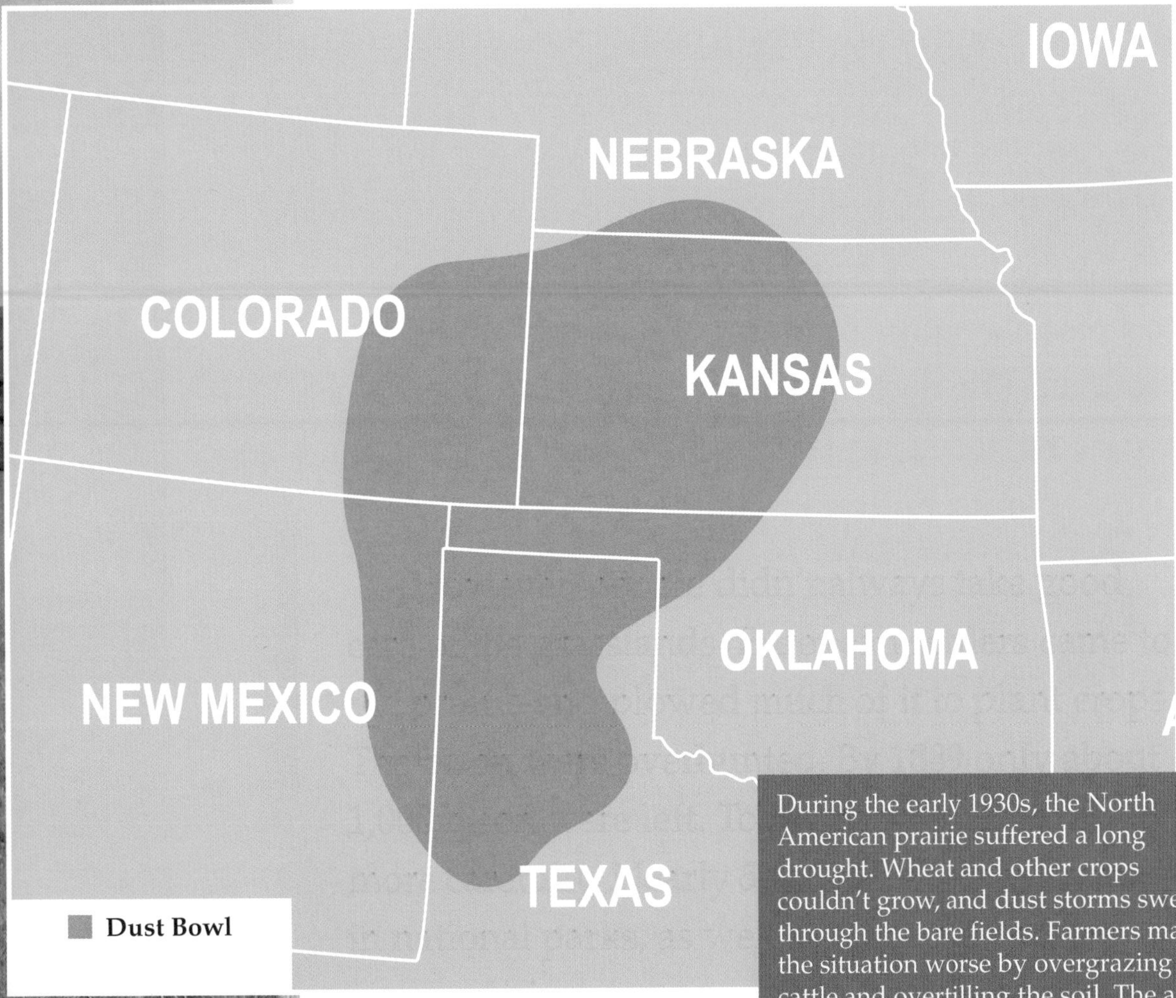

IOWA

NEBRASKA

COLORADO

KANSAS

NEW MEXICO

OKLAHOMA

TEXAS

■ Dust Bowl

During the early 1930s, the North American prairie suffered a long drought. Wheat and other crops couldn't grow, and dust storms swept through the bare fields. Farmers made the situation worse by overgrazing cattle and overtilling the soil. The area was called the Dust Bowl.

THE FUTURE OF GRASSLAND BIOMES

People can do many things to help save grasslands. Some farmers rotate crops. The farmers plant a different crop each growing season to help the soil keep more nutrients. To hold soil in place, farmers plant strips of native grasses next to fields.

Many people plant grassland flowers in neighborhoods and cities. The flowers attract colorful butterflies that flutter between flowers, pollinating as they go. These gardens help preserve bees and other insects. Bees can thrive if people use fewer chemicals.

In the United States, some national parks work to preserve native prairie. The Tallgrass Prairie National Preserve in Kansas is one example of these parks. Restoring and preserving prairies can bring back native plants, butterflies, and bees.

FACT BOX

What can you do? Everyone can help bring the grasslands back into balance. Healthy soil is one important part of the grassland biome. You can help make healthy soil by composting. During this process, natural material such as leaves, grass, and vegetable peelings are decomposed and recycled into rich soil. You can even add worms to speed up the recycling process. Check books or composting websites, ask an adult to help choose a compost bin, and get started!

An urban garden in Chicago features native grassland plants.

Grasslands are fragile. But by working together, we will be able to enjoy the benefits of grasslands for years to come.

GLOSSARY

adapt (uh-DAPT)—to adjust to particular conditions
or plant to better fit its environment is called an adaptation

aphid (AY-fuhd)—a tiny bug that sucks sap from plants

carnivore (KAHR-nuh-vohr)—an animal that eats only meat

decomposer (dee-kuhm-PO-zur)—a living thing that breaks down
natural material

dormant (DOR-muhnt)—when growth slows down or stops

drought (DROUT)—a long period of weather with little or no rain

dung (DUHNG)—solid waste from animals

endangered (in-DAYN-juhrd)—at risk of dying out

graze (GRAYZ)—to eat grass and other plants

guanaco (gwah-NAH-koh)—an animal resembling a llama that lives in
the pampas

herbivore (HUR-buh-vor)—an animal that eats only plants

irrigate (IHR-uh-gate)—to supply water to crops using pipes or channels

migration (mye-GRAY-shuhn)—the regular movement of animals as
they search different places for food

nomad (NOH-mad)—a person who moves from place to place to find
food and water, rather than living in one spot

nutrient (NOO-tree-uhnt)—a substance that plants and animals need for
good health

pollinator (POL-uh-nayt-uhr)—a living thing that moves pollen from
one part of a plant to another, allowing the plant to form seeds

scavenger (SKAV-uhn-jer)—a living thing that eats dead or rotting animals

READ MORE

Gregory, Josh. *African Savanna.* Community Connections. Ann Arbor, MI: Cherry Lake Publishing, 2016.

Owings, Lisa. *From Garbage to Compost.* Start to Finish. Minneapolis: Lerner Publications, 2017.

Royston, Angela. *Grassland Food Chains.* Food Chains and Webs. Chicago: Heinemann Library, 2015.

INTERNET SITES

Grasslands
http://www.blueplanetbiomes.org/grasslands.htm

Plant a Butterfly Garden
https://climatekids.nasa.gov/butterfly-garden

Wildebeest Migration
https://www.nationalgeographic.org/media/wildebeest-migration/

U.N. Urges Eating Insects: 8 Popular Bugs to Try
https://news.nationalgeographic.com/news/2013/13/130514-edible-insects-entomophagy-science-food-bugs-beetles/

CRITICAL THINKING QUESTIONS

1. Elephant, pampas, and other prairie grasses have very deep roots. How might these help clean water that flows underground?
2. Grasslands are good for wind energy. With wide-open skies, what other form of renewable energy might work well in grasslands?
3. How do you think an increasing human population will affect grasslands?

INDEX